Battling to See God's Glory

PASTOR MELVIN KNIGHT

ISBN 979-8-89428-775-1 (paperback)
ISBN 979-8-89428-776-8 (digital)

Copyright © 2024 by Pastor Melvin Knight

All rights reserved. No part of this publication may be reproduced, distributed, or transmitted in any form or by any means, including photocopying, recording, or other electronic or mechanical methods without the prior written permission of the publisher. For permission requests, solicit the publisher via the address below.

Christian Faith Publishing
832 Park Avenue
Meadville, PA 16335
www.christianfaithpublishing.com

Printed in the United States of America

To my wife of thirty-six years, Gwength.
To the memory of our daughter, Kewondra.
God has been good to me.

Purpose

The purpose of this short book is to help those who are going through hard times or who have gone through discouraging times.

Main Audience

This book is geared toward any individual who may or may not have experienced multiple challenges and faced grief, or in other words, it is for the ones who have been there and done that.[1]

Guiding scriptures:
- Matthew 5:4
- Joshua 1:9
- Psalm 73:26
- 2 Corinthians 4:17–18
- Revelations 21:4

---

[1] Someone may use this expression to indicate that they have had a similar experience, and therefore, the experience is not unique or unknown to them. "Been There Done That (Got the T-shirt)," Collins COBUILD, accessed April 29, 2024, https://www.collinsdictionary.com/dictionary/english/been-there-done-that.

CONTENTS

Preface ix
Chapter 1: Introduction 1
Chapter 2: Three Phases 5
    Phase 1: The Beginning 5
    Phase 2: The Test 8
    Phase 3: Results 15
Chapter 3: Conclusion 17
Afterword 19
Bibliography 21

PREFACE

God bless you! I say it from a heart that knows we are already blessed, and we need only remind ourselves and others that we are blessed. Even as our hearts and flesh fail, God has never failed us (Psalm 73:26 KJV). With that knowledge, I write this book and share it with you because God blessed me and wants me to share this blessing.

This short book is intended to strongly encourage you to stop complaining, if that is what you tend to do when you face hardship or pains. As difficult as it may be to not complain, it is important to put your mind to resist the urge or habit to complain and yield to the temptation to let depression continue to guide you to low spiritual, mental, and physical valleys. The God, Most High, that you say you believe in will go with you through everyday tests of your strength, faith, character, and courage, but you must be willing to go with God's leading to higher places. The God that you say you believe in has already blessed you to overcome, but you must accept the blessing and go with God.

Knowing who God is and what God has already done will help you face difficulties and will also help you seek ways to understand and gain wisdom. Wisdom is a glorious gift from God! In our seasons of stressful testing, we would do well to consider what we already know, have already learned, and believe in our hearts. What we come to believe and know in our hearts, we can confess from our souls, with our mouths.

First of all, we know when our hearts are being tested. We are not ignorant. Secondly, we know that tests occur not just to see if we will pass or fail, but also to see if we will continue trying and not give up. We are aware. As we try to withstand these tests, we have to grow stronger and wiser, which means we have to get in better condition or better shape. We have to get strong enough to endure. The gift of wisdom makes us strong and confident in the knowledge that comes from God, not from man.

We all know what a gym or gymnasium is, don't we? A gym is a facility made for workout purposes, a place to train so that we can become healthy and strong enough to resist or fight enemies to our souls and bodies. The more we train and fight, the more ribbons and bars we can earn and also the more scars we can suffer.

One day, you and I will be called to stand before God, who hopefully will say to you, "Well *done,* good and faithful servant… Enter into the joy of your Lord" (Holy Bible, King James Version). The joy of our Lord is a place of rest to enter when we have shown ourselves faithful.

Again, I say, God bless you! As you read these words of my testimony, may they add to your life more encouragement to endure whatever difficult tests you must complete before you stand before God and wait for the evaluation. God bless you as you work and while you wait.

CHAPTER 1

Introduction

Without the power to turn and walk or run away from this life, my wife, Gwength, and I have had to stand in place. Even when we wanted to sit down, lie down, and at times, when we were ready to give up and die, we could not make such moves. Instead, we have had to get up many times, let go of our feelings, and follow the instructions of God, regardless of how we *felt*. We have had to be as soldiers, required to continue to stand and serve during difficult battles.

Looking back at God's instructions has helped me to continue to get up, especially when I wanted to give up or stay down. Looking back at God's instructions has helped my wife and me to recall certain sad situations and see that as sorrowful as they were, and sometimes still make us *feel*, those situations were not meant to punish us. Even those sad situations reminded us that they were also intermingled with some of the most blessed times in our individual lives and in our life as a married couple and family. In other words, in spite of our sorrows, God has blessed my wife and me to continue to remember that *God's glory* will be the final outcome despite the battles, suffering, and sadness we face in this physical life.[2] God's victory is assured, and therefore, we as God's creations and children

---

[2] "Blessed are they that mourn: for they shall be comforted" (Matthew 5:4, King James Version, Holy Bible).

must also be assured in the knowledge and belief that we are blessed even as we face sorrows.

Here, I will tell you and show you what I mean when I use the word *blessed*. A blessed person is someone that God has gifted with favor in life.[3] The blessings of God can come in unique wrappings, and at times, we do not expect to receive them. I can say that July 3, 1989, was a blessed day for my wife and me, for on that day, God blessed my wife and me with a wonderful baby girl that we named Kewondra. In fact, Gwength and her sister Wanda came up with a beautiful name for our wonderful, unique daughter.

When I use the word *wonderful* to describe Kewondra, I mean that Kewondra was never a problem. She was an inspiration and joy to be around. She brought happiness to my life and family for so many reasons, including because she was smart, obedient, talented, and loving. I truly mean it when I say that this child grew up to show me that God was not through with me! God was not through blessing me with favor and happiness.

Not only was Kewondra a great daughter, but she was also my devoted friend and companion who treated my wife and me as blessings to her life. Kewondra told my wife something my wife cannot forget, and neither can I. She told my wife that she did not want to "outlive" us, her mother and me. She said she would prefer to go home with the Lord before we passed because she did not want to live in this world without us. Such words from a child's mouth sound loving on the one hand, but on the other hand, they are concerning to a parent. No parent wants to think of their children to pass away at any time, but especially not before the children have certain life experiences. Definitely, no loving parent wants to be left behind to face the loss of their children and the grief.

A Rocky Start

Kewondra was a blessing to my wife and me. In spite of the blessed addition of our daughter to our family and other blessings,

---

[3] Definition 2 of *blessed*, "divinely or happily favored" (Dictionary.com).

my wife and I had a rocky start to our marriage, which made it challenging at first to see all the blessings of God. With God's help and guidance, we made it through some tough times and remained together. To stay together, we had to let God take control of our individual lives and take control over our marital life. As we began to let God take control of our lives, my wife and I thought life would get much easier. However, life became harder once we decided to turn our lives over to God's control. It became clear to me as time passed that our tests were never going to be easy tests. We would have to study, so study we did.

As my study life continued to develop, I began to remember what my mother used to say while we were in the fields chopping weeds. My mother was a strong woman of faith, and she would make statements such as, "I won't always be here to help you, so you're going to have to trust God." At that time, I was a young man of about fifteen years of age; therefore, I did not grasp the full meaning of trusting God. As a young man, I also did not know I would have to pass through phases that would build my genuine trust in God, teach me to trust God with all my problems, yet also test my trust in God. When I was a child, I didn't realize or think about the battles, tests, and trials I would have to face in order to become a stronger soldier battling to see God's glory, and I wasn't aware that God had already predestined my life battles, tests, and trials to bring me to this place of battling.

Soldiers have to study and learn how to see. We soldiers have to learn how to view life and all its conflicts, battles, and wars with the vision God has given us. We have to study as part of our training so that as we go through different situations, we do not get so frightened, confused, or depressed that we give up hope and accept defeat. We have to keep learning how to be hopeful and faithful, because that is what will keep our eyes from closing in despair.

I hope that by reading this book, you will find what I also found to be true—that God is concerned with all our problems. God's eyes are open to our human issues and pains. My wife brings to memory often, and even during the drafting of this book, the scripture from 2 Corinthians 4:17–18 (King James Version, Holy Bible):

> For our light affliction, which is but for a moment, worketh for us a far more exceeding and eternal weight of glory; while we look not at the things which are seen, but at the things which are not seen: for the things which are seen are temporal; but the things which are not seen are eternal.

To help you understand this message, I ask you to focus on these three steps or phases: (1) the Beginning, (2) the Test, and (3) the Results. These were the phases I experienced while battling to witness God's glory that will be revealed despite times of great sorrow and tribulation.

CHAPTER 2

Three Phases

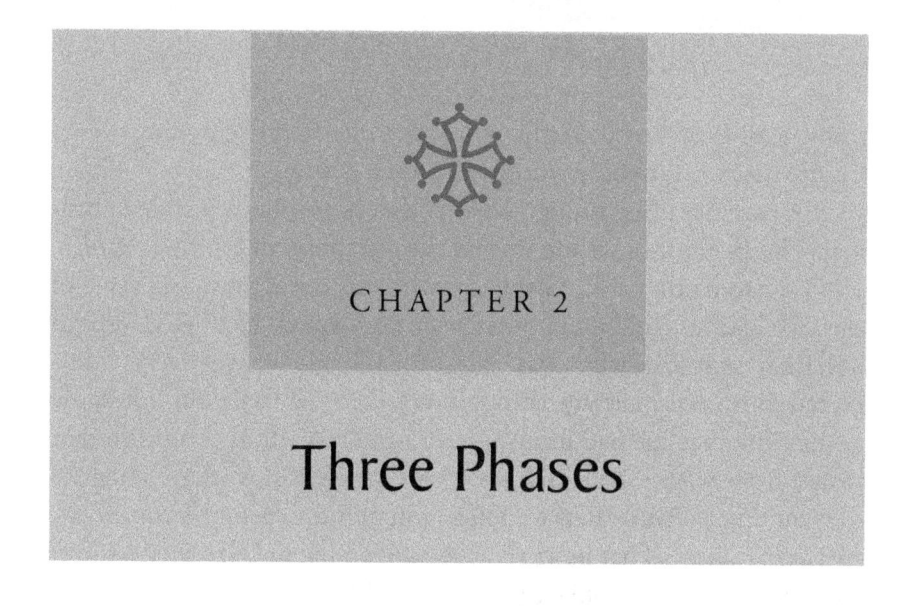

One dictionary definition of the word *phase* is that it is a "distinguishable part in a course, development, or cycle."[4] While developing my trust in God, I went through the following three phases: (1) the Beginning, (2) the Test, and (3) the Results. As you gain understanding of these three phases, I hope you will learn that even in difficulty, God's glory will be revealed. Perhaps you, too, will be a witness to God's power to guide us through grief and loss experiences.

Phase 1: The Beginning

Many paths are uncharted.[5] Therefore, many people are frightened to set out on an unchartered path. For others, an unchartered path thrills them, because they like adventure and challenges. Some people look forward to looking back one day and saying that they traveled a pathway and that they have become the voice of experience because they have been there and done that. As for the "been there, done that" crowd, I don't need to talk to you as much. At this point, I

---

[4] Definition of *phase* (*Merriam-Webster*, America's Most Trusted Dictionary).
[5] *Uncharted*, Dictionary.com, accessed April 29, 2024, https://www.dictionary.com/browse/uncharted.

really need to talk to and help people experiencing frightening events for the first time, people who have not *been there*.

A path has a beginning, whether that beginning is visible or hidden. The Beginning for me was on the afternoon of Sunday, April 3, 1988. I had a new bride, Gwength, who was only twenty-six years of age. We had no children, and we were very green. Neither Gwength nor I had any idea what was ahead for us, but we were very determined to see our marriage through its course. My wife did not know at the time that she had lupus, a very serious medical condition that would limit where she could work and the type of work or activities she could perform. When we found out about Gwength's condition, we had to adjust. That news put pressure on me to help carry out our daily duties, and of course, Gwength did her share. However, what kind of husband would ask of his wife to give any more than she is able to give? Not a good one, I can tell you.

My wife and I prayed and continued to trust God in the matter. We spent time trying to figure it (life) out, while believing that God would see us through. We decided to move forward, and at this time, God gave us our baby girl, little Kewondra Gwenita Knight. Over the course of the nine months that Gwength carried our baby in her womb, I made up my mind and began to do more to help provide for our family.

My work history had involved me serving time in the military in the mid-1970s to the early 1980s. By the late 1980s, as a new husband with a new baby, I was working two jobs. To supplement my family's income, I decided to join the National Guard. Soon after I joined the National Guard, in 1990, and with a young wife and child at home, I was called to active duty and sent to serve in the first Persian Gulf War.[6] I had just come home for Thanksgiving, in 1990, when I was called to the war. It was a very worry-filled time, of course, as I wondered what my wife would do without me around.

---

[6] The Persian Gulf War, first phase, was Operation Desert Shield; it lasted from August 2, 1990, to January 17, 1991, according to the following source: US Navy, "The Gulf War 1990–1991 (Operation Desert Shield/ Desert Storm)," Naval History and Heritage Command.

All of these new, uncharted paths in my life brought with them much stress. At that point, God really had to help me!

We should thank all military personnel for their many sacrifices for our country. On February 16, 1991, we (troops) were on our way to war in what was named Operation Desert Storm or Desert Shield. For some crazy reason, I started using drugs and alcohol.

When I returned home after a year of active duty, I found it hard to adjust. I was angry all the time. I felt a great deal of physical and mental pain, and I did not know how to handle it well. Drugs and alcohol seemed to help me ease the pain I was experiencing. However, the trade-off was that my marriage began to suffer. My attempts to manage my issues through drug and alcohol caused more problems, and it reached the point that I could not stand to see what my wife and daughter were having to go through, or rather what I was putting them through.

I remember one Sunday morning as I was taking my wife and daughter to church, my wife just broke down and started screaming, in tears, saying, "I will not put me and my baby through this." Something snapped in me that day. It hurt me to my core to hear my wife's anguish and to know that I was the main reason she was so frustrated and hurt. I knew then that I had to improve my spiritual, physical, and mental health problems.

At that time, I began to focus on improving my spiritual condition. I assumed everybody in the church was in a relationship with God; therefore, I started going back to church, with the expectation that I would develop a relationship with God. I actually found some comfort in returning to church, though that comfort did not last long. Also, during that time, my wife had a business that she had done very well operating. I began helping her with the business, and also, I began getting some assistance with my health issues from the Veterans Administration (VA). We were starting to get on a better track, and finally, things began looking up.

For the first time, my life was *fine*. My wife, daughter, and I began to travel. We truly enjoyed exploring new places and spending time together as a family. We were considered middle class, and we were enjoying life. We were even able to afford to purchase brand-new vehicles, and we lived comfortably, at least for a few years.

This beginning, as difficult as it was, was my new foundation for learning what a soul needs in order to continue through difficulties. What does a soul need? Well, I learned what I want you to learn, which is that a soul needs to be very careful and prayerful when life is going well and when we are having positive experiences. I learned as well that you must be just as careful and prayerful when life is filled with harsh experiences and not going so well. In other words, we should always be careful and prayerful and to do as the Bible instructs: we are "to watch and pray" (Matthew 26:41 KJV).

I am a firm believer in God's word. In Matthew 26:57 (KJV), we encounter a man named Jesus who was led from one court to another to answer for crimes he did not commit. Jesus was not guilty; nevertheless, the courts had already convicted him. *Does that sound like the experience of anyone you know?* Sometimes, the enemy takes us through trials, one after the other. The enemy's objective is to heap so much pressure on us that we begin to feel so hopeless. In our hopeless state, we plead *guilty*, even when we are *not guilty*.

Pleading guilty when you are not guilty is the same as giving up or quitting. Please do not give up on your defense. You have the best defense, a defense that money can never retain, and that defense is heavenly. Your lawyer in heaven has never lost a case and never will. He knows our infirmities, our conscience, our souls. That is why we should just trust our lawyer God, because God will never abandon us. When we start to love God for *who* God is and not for *what* he does for us, we begin to see and *relate* to God on another level. When we start to see God and relate to him, we begin to witness the glorious nature and goodness of God and we can witness to others.

Phase 2: The Test

If phase 1 is the beginning and foundation phase, then phase 2 is the testing phase. We know what a test is. A test is the opportunity for us to prove what we know or have learned. Minister Thomas Tarrants of the C. S. Lewis Institute defined the word *test* from a biblical perspective, and generally, he showed that a test is a situation meant to show what is within a person or what a person needs to gain. Minister Tarrants explains it this way:

> A test is a situation that God sends or allows in our life with the intention of revealing our loyalties, motivations, character, and commitment to Him and [for] helping to purify, strengthen, and mature us. If successfully passed, a test also glorifies God.[7]

Here, we see it stated as clear as day. If we pass our tests, then God gets the glory!

The Minefield

During phase 2, or my testing phase, I started to experience a whole new level of suffering that I had never seen before. I was failing from the start, and I knew this was ground that I had never before treaded. I thought about all the loved ones and friends who had passed away. I thought of my father passing away, my mother passing away, my brother passing away, and my sister passing away. Then, three close friends of mine passed away. Seeing so many of my loved ones passing away made me think that the next steps I took were critical ones. Because *death* had shown me how quickly and sometimes quietly it moves, I began to consider that the next life to pass away could be mine, me.

Seriously, I began to reflect more on life because death had made its visitations so frequently. Death's frequency made me aware that the ground I was treading was a minefield.[8] In military language, a minefield is a dangerous area wherein many explosives (mines) are set and can be triggered. In civilian terms, a minefield is a place to

---

[7] Thomas A. Tarrants, "Temptation and Testing," C. S. Lewis Institute.
[8] *Minefield*, Dictionary.com, accessed May 4, 2024, https://www.dictionary.com/ browse /minefield.

tread through carefully, because a wrong movement, or without any warning or a sign, a dangerous or devastating situation can happen. Though I faced a spiritual minefield, I look back and realize that the minefield I faced was also my testing ground.

Life's Meaning

When Kewondra, my beautiful, unique daughter, was two years old, her favorite song was called "What's the Meaning of Life."[9] She loved that song and would get happy when it played. Early in her growth, I noticed that she was a very special and genuinely loving child. Kewondra very much loved us as her parents, and we loved her, too, and did all we could to make her life as happy as we knew how to make it.

Remember I stated that my wife was diagnosed with lupus. At the time of her diagnosis, times were very challenging, especially as she was going in and out of hospitals and from doctor to doctor.

---

[9] Unknown artist or lyricist.

Sometimes, I felt it was unfair that Gwength was facing so many health challenges. It was a tough situation, watching someone I love experience so many pains. At that time, also, I did not know God as well as I would come to know him; therefore, I did not understand why God allowed so much pain in some people's lives.

Later, my wife and I would get more bad news. Our daughter was also diagnosed with lupus. This news was devastating, and all I could think was, *Here we go again!* Next, I wondered, *Where do we go from here?* The answer was we go to God, of course, and also, we go back to the doctors, but this time with my baby girl.

For a while, Kewondra's condition did not get any better. However, as her health eventually permitted, Gwength and I started taking Kewondra places we had never been together. One place I took my family was to New York. We even went to a Broadway play to see *The Color Purple*, starring Fantasia. That was an exciting experience that I was so happy to be able to share with my wife and daughter.

My family and I also visited Nashville, Tennessee, to enjoy our favorite barbecue house, and we went to New Orleans to eat gumbo. Our traveling was extensive, as we also traveled to Atlanta, to Spondivits restaurant, which was one of our favorite spots, as well as to Birmingham, Alabama, to Pappadeaux Seaford Kitchen, and to Orlando and Tampa, Florida, just to eat and experience life to the fullest.

The last trip we took together was to Fort Walton Beach, Florida. Kewondra was relying on an oxygen tank at that time. We had no idea that we only had three months left with her before Kewondra would graduate from this life to go be with the Lord.

Oh, how Kewondra's passing broke my heart! When the time came for her to go home with God, I cried, and I cried for two solid years. She passed away on August 6, 2020, but not due to the pandemic of 2020,[10] as some might think. My daughter passed away because lupus attacked her heart and lungs. Ironically, Kewondra's driver's license expired the same day she passed!

---

[10] The COVID-19 or coronavirus pandemic of 2020.

When a parent buries a child like this, it is not easy. I did not want to get out of bed. Kewondra passed away that Thursday night, August 6, 2020. Friday, August 7, 2020, was the worst day of my life. I thought I felt bad when my father, mother, brother, sister, and three close friends passed away; however, their passing did not hold a candle[11] to what I was about to go through after Kewondra passed on to glory.

After Kewondra's funeral services, I was a walking zombie. I felt that I was deceased. I did not care about anything except my wife, who had given me such a wonderful human being to help raise. It had been such a pleasure to have someone in my life to help me come to know God better. Kewondra added so much light to my life. I even commented that she was more than my child, because often she seemed to know exactly what I was feeling or thinking. She understood and encouraged me.

After all that my wife and I had experienced, it was as if I could still hear my baby saying, "Daddy, keep up the good works you started." You see, before she got to where she could no longer go places, we had a small Bible study group that she enjoyed. I called off the Bible study in order to see about my wife and child. However, to the end, Kewondra glorified God. While not feeling well, she sang songs of praise, and one of her memorable social media videos was of her singing and giving God her best gift, a sacrificial praise. She passed the tests, and God received the glory!

Here, I would like to say these words to you who believe you can have your best life now: You could probably have a "good time," but you will not have your "best life" if you are not seeking and following God with all your heart. When we come to God with an open heart and an understanding of his truth over or above our own truth, we find out that this life is God's doing and not our doing. To have our best life, we must give up our ways and our desires to just have a good time. Giving up our own ways and desires may be a challenge,

---

[11] Gary Martin expression believed to originate in the 1600s and indicates that nothing closely resembles or compares to the experience or situation.

and following God's way of doing or being may feel like a great sacrifice; however, in the long run, it is worth the sacrifice.

Battle after Battle

When we experience life-changing moments and tests such as what I and many others have experienced, it is good to know that we will pass those tests with God. My older sister, Grace, and my wife, Gwength, became my top motivators, along with the memory of my encouraging daughter, Kewondra. They have all at some point encouraged me to keep hanging on every time hard times have come. They have often told me to go back into "the battle."

Many times, I wanted to just throw my hands up and quit. I could feel my child telling me to press on. I could also hear my sister Grace saying, "Press on." I could also hear my wife saying, "Press on." My wife, in particular, motivated me to continue to stay in the race and reminded me of this scripture: "The race is not given to the swift nor the battle to the strong" (Ecclesiastes 9:11 KJV). The ones who finish the race and endure the battle are the ones who pass the tests. The ones who pass the tests are the ones who glorify God!

While experiencing life's battles, I thought about Job many more times than I can count. In the book of Job, in the Holy Bible, it was God who asked Satan if he had "considered" testing the fortitude and faith of his servant Job. Sometimes, it seems that everything comes against us. Well, if you do not have a relationship with God, you could lose your mind when you feel one problem or attack or sorrow after another comes.

I had so many emotions going on at the same time as I experienced test after test after test. I remember how I felt, and I also remember that my wife was not talking much. She was just grieving in her own way while I was so disconnected while grieving in my own way. Sometimes, she and I both just took life one day at a time, not knowing what to expect next.

One year later, after our daughter's passing, I was stricken with a condition called motor neuron disease, a condition I have battled for a few years now. This disease destroys the nerves and muscles in the body and began attacking my legs. I started to fall often. Just like a rock, I would just sink. My doctor asked if while in the military I had served in any areas where there were burn pits. The answer was yes, I had served in such areas, but I will not go much further into detail regarding that situation. This condition is similar to what is referred to as ALS.[12]

Because of motor neuron disease, I sometimes had to look down at my feet just to figure out what position or direction my feet were in. I also would have to ask my wife to move my feet from one position to another for me, because I could not physically move them myself. As you know, I love to travel, but as you may guess, I lost the ability to drive, which limited my ability to travel. I began to question God, asking, "What next?"

At this point, I begged God to take my life. I cried so much. It was unbelievable to me that I had gone through so much heartache and adversity, especially in such a short span of time as nine months. Then, as if what I had already suffered had not been enough, even more suffering arrived.

On the morning of June 22, 2022, I attempted to get out of my recliner in order to get in my wheelchair. As I made this maneuver, I suddenly fell backward in my recliner. In that instance, I felt that my wish for God to take my life had come true. I thought I was going where my baby was.

I was taken to the emergency room where medical staff gave me an intravenous (IV) drip to hydrate me. Doctors then sent me home. Later that night, I started to sweat as though someone had poured water on me. My wife called for the emergency medical services, and they took me to a better hospital.

At the more advanced hospital, I received an additional diagnosis and learned I had suffered a stroke and a heart attack on the same day. I underwent treatment and stayed in the hospital for a month. After I was released from the hospital, I was admitted to a rehabilitation center. Following my stay in rehab, my attitude changed. I now wanted to continue here in this life and finish my course, especially

---

[12] Amyotrophic lateral sclerosis (ALS).

for my wife. She had already told me that she wanted me to stop talking of dying and start talking of living. I understood that meant I had to change my words, if I was going to survive the testing.

For a year or more now, I have focused more on living. Sometimes, I have to fight a little harder to function, but each day, I keep fighting. I keep battling. I remember what I went through, the stress and grief. I also reflect on all the wonderful times God let me enjoy with my baby, wife, and all my loved ones, even though many have passed on.

When I reflect, I begin to worship God for who he is. While in worship, God has shown me the question he posed to Satan: "Have you considered my servant Melvin?" God showed me that he loved me in spite of my shortcomings and that he allowed me to be tested. I know that God loves me, after bringing me through all the testing that I have gone through. To God goes the glory!

Phase 3: Results

After the testing comes the result phase or phase 3. If you finish and pass your test, then your result will be good. Throughout the Word of God, we see him evaluate using the word *good*, as in good things, good gifts, and good years! We then can see that what is good can also be acceptable.

If we do our best to do good for God and produce good results, God will uphold us. If we stay faithful to his call, we are doing good. We never have to wonder where God is once we come through our test. Remember this: You are more aware of what surrounds you once you reach the end of your test. You will also feel more grateful. You will feel better, and your best life is in view.

If you do not know something that would help you finish and pass your test, then ask questions. People who say, "Do not question God," need to read more. If your children ask you a question, do you chastise them? No, you answer them. In the Holy Bible, there was Adam, Eve, Abraham, Sarah, Moses, David, Elijah, John the Baptist, and the list goes on. Even Jesus had questions. There is no sin in asking questions. Just know that God can answer them all, no matter how much you do not understand. God understands the tests may be difficult, but he also understands that he is the one able to keep you and me from failing and falling (Jude 1:24 KJV). Hold and lean on to God!

CHAPTER 3

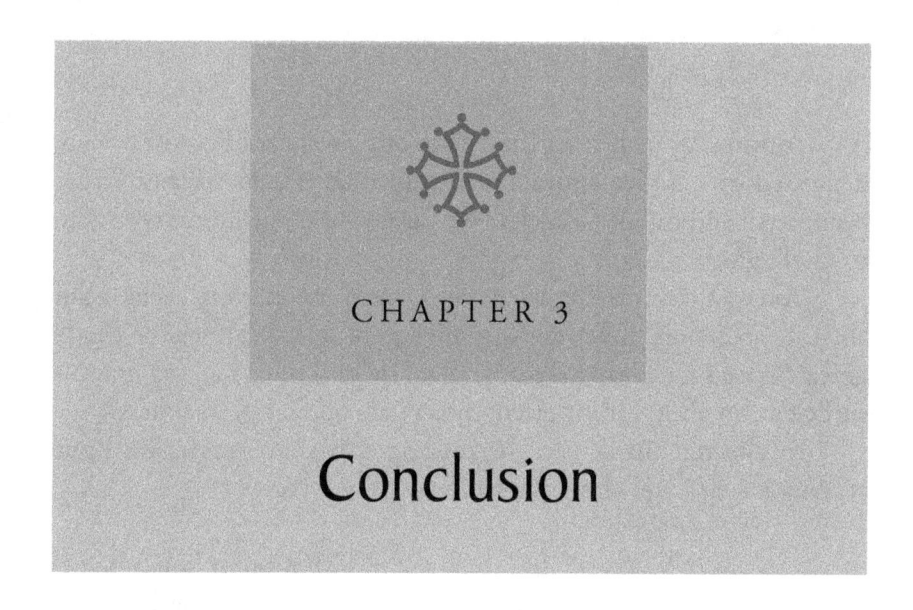

Conclusion

From the beginning, it seemed *we* were chosen *to be put* through tests. When I use the word *we*, I am talking about my wife and myself, but I am also talking about other humans similar to us, who face life's challenges and wonder if they (we) will survive. I am talking about all of us, who have faced difficult tests.

Enduring tests requires tested humans to seek and gain superhuman strength at times. That strength comes from God, when we trust him to provide it. It is strange to think that when we feel most weak, we need to demonstrate the greatest strength, character, maturity. To many people, it seems impossible to be strong when you feel so weak and in such battles; however, "all things are possible with God" (Matthew 19:26 KJV). God is the one who gives us superhuman strength when we need it.

God has the answers, too. We are instructed to study and prayerfully seek God's help. Therefore, keep believing you will pass your test as long as you keep trying and keep giving all glory to God! Keep the hope in your heart alive! Never stop dreaming! Always know that you cannot out-sin God's love, and "where sin abounded, grace did much more abound" (Romans 5:20–21 KJV). That means that no matter what you have done, you can ask God to forgive you.

According to the Bible, all humans have sinned and fallen short of God's glory(Romans 3:23–24). That means all of us have failed some test. What keeps us from failing the entire course of life is us continuing to live and not take our own lives because we are depressed or sad. We also are not to give up on life because it has been harsh and full of obstacles. We cannot stop battling as witnesses to God's glory.

Today, I have feeling in my legs, and I am moving them. I am alive. I am living, functioning evidence of and a witness to God's grace! Second Corinthians reads, "And he said unto me, my grace is sufficient for thee: for my strength is made perfect in weakness."

In closing, thank you for reading this short book. We hope reading it helps you along the pathway to heaven.

With love, in Jesus's name,
Brother Melvin and Sister Gwength Knight

AFTERWORD

People who have gone through so many battles and storms need empathy and encouragement. They are the survivors of battles and storms, some of which may have taken from them loved ones that they deeply miss. This world gives wars and storms different names so that we can go back later and talk about the damages they left behind and the lives (young and elderly) that they took. Generally, however, we can say that the battles and storms that many of us have survived fall under the big umbrella term or general label *grief*.

Many of us have grieved, and our tears have rained down, maybe even stormed down. Under the watchful and caring eye of our Father God, many of us have cried, and at times, we have even fallen down on our knees and begged God to help us make it through difficult seasons full of tests. We have cried and begged God to either stop the pains or take us out of this world. All we really had to do, however, was give God our hearts, for he promised to wipe away tears and bring new order (Revelations 21:4).

Many people have suffered while grieving, because they have, while in the process of grieving, also fell and felt physically, emotionally, mentally, and spiritually hurt and suffered. When we as people are hurting, we are not always aware that we are not the only ones hurting or suffering. We also forget that we are not alone, even though we feel like we have been abandoned in our hours of grief and pain. That is why it is good to have positive people around us to remind us to keep going and urge us to speak of life rather than of death.

As you think about what you read in this book, remember that you are not alone, even if you cannot physically reach out and touch that loved one who has gone home with God. Remember also that during the toughest tests, do all in your power to recall God's instructions and promises in his Word. Even as we dread opening our eyes because we can no longer physically view or touch the people we want to view or touch, we still have to open our eyes and determine to look forward to seeing God and what God has promised us. We still have to stay in touch with God.

Dear friends, God did not allow us to be born into this earth and allow us to see daylight just so that we give up, shut our eyes, and retreat into dark places. Actually, during our most difficult and darkest tests and times, we have the instruction to lift our eyes off the situation here on the ground and lift our vision above sorrow-filled situations. With our eyes lifted, we can see more accurately. We can see that we have not been left to drown in lowly places called sorrow and grief. With our eyes lifted, our vision is rightly positioned to see that God is our ever-faithful help. Also, especially when we feel most helpless, depressed, and tested, the glory of God shall be revealed, and we are God's witnesses.

Thank you for reading.

BIBLIOGRAPHY

Albert, David, and Daniel Gamm, eds. "Fanny Crosby." *Encyclopedia Britannica*. Last modified July 20, 1998. https://www.britannica.com/biography/Fanny-Crosby.

"Been There Done That (Got the T-shirt)." Collins COBUILD, publisher. Accessed April 29, 2024./english/been-there-done-that.

Bible Hub. Accessed May 26, 2024. https://biblehub.com/jude/1-24.htm.

Blessed. Meanings and Definitions of English Words. Dictionary.com. Accessed May 25, 2024. https://www.dictionary.com/browse/blessed.

Minefield. Dictionary.com. Accessed May 4, 2024. https://www.dictionary.com/bro wse/minefield.

Phase. Definition of *phase*. Merriam-Webster: America's Most Trusted Dictionary. Last modified May 20, 2024. https://www.merriamwebster.com/dictionary/phase.

Tarrants, Thomas A. "Temptation and Testing." C. S. Lewis Institute. Last modified April 20, 2024. https://www.cslewisinstitute.org.

Uncharted. Dictionary.com. Accessed April 29, 2024. https://www.dictionary.com/browse/uncharted.

US Navy. "The Gulf War 1990–1991 (Operation Desert Shield/Desert Storm)." Naval History and Heritage Command. Accessed April 26, 2024. https://www.history.navy.mil/our-collect ions/art/exhibits/conflicts-and-operations/the-gulf-war-1990-1991--operation-desert-shield--desert-storm.html.

ABOUT THE AUTHOR

Melvin Knight Jr. has been married to his wife, Gwength H. Knight, for thirty-six years. This book was written in memory of their daughter, Kewondra G. Knight, who has given them so much joy and happiness. Melvin doesn't have a lot to say about himself, but he shares, "Glory to God who has made it possible for me to write this book in belief that this book blesses everyone who reads it. God bless."

Printed in the USA
CPSIA information can be obtained
at www.ICGtesting.com
LVHW021242301124
797959LV00001B/224